The Art of Photojournalism Wedding Photography

Hector M. Melendez

Copyright © 2020 Hector M. Melendez All rights reserved

No part of this book may be reproduced, or stored in a retrieval system, or transmitted in any form or by any means, electronic, mechanical, photocopying, recording, or otherwise, without express written permission of the publisher.

Printed in the United States of America

CONTENTS

Title Page

Copyright

Introduction

Photojournalistic Style

Preparation

At the Bride's House

Groom

Ceremony

Reception

Children

Action

Moments

Other Events

Light

Tips for Taking Great Photos

Equipment

Contingency Planning

Editing

Final Product

INTRODUCTION

My interest in photography began with landscapes. Being a resident of the Caribbean island of Puerto Rico and having as many beautiful landscapes as beaches, tropical forests, rivers, and mountains, helped me develop my eye for this art.

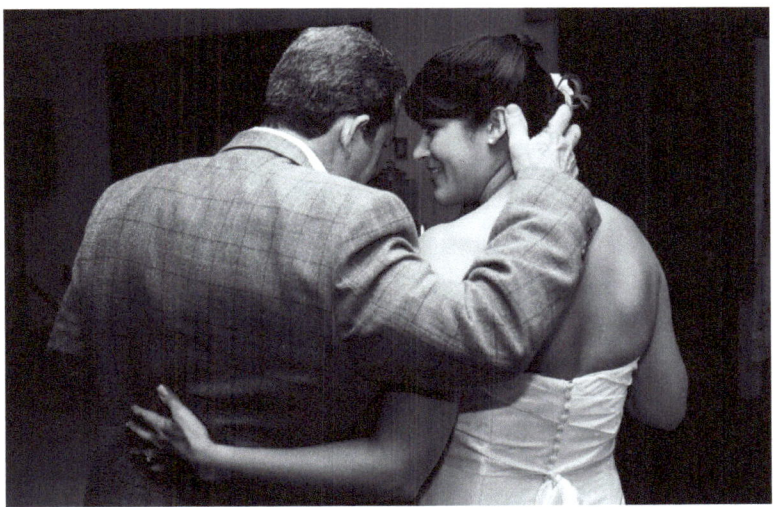

It was not until the birth of my first child that I entered the world of photography, my children being the best motivation to read books, take courses and practice. I decided to practice with my friends' weddings and in a short time I began to be referred to work for other people, this being my starting point in the wedding photography business.

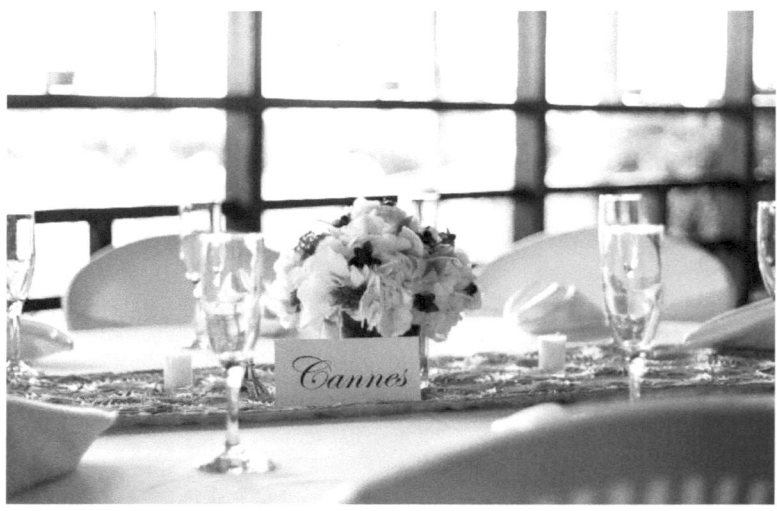

In this book I share my techniques for taking great wedding photos in a journalistic style. This book is for people with a basic understanding of photography. I recommend that people who are starting to use a DSLR camera buy a basic photography book and learn first how to use their camera in manual mode. I hope you enjoy and learn by reading this book, and start taking great images.

PHOTOJOURNALISTIC STYLE

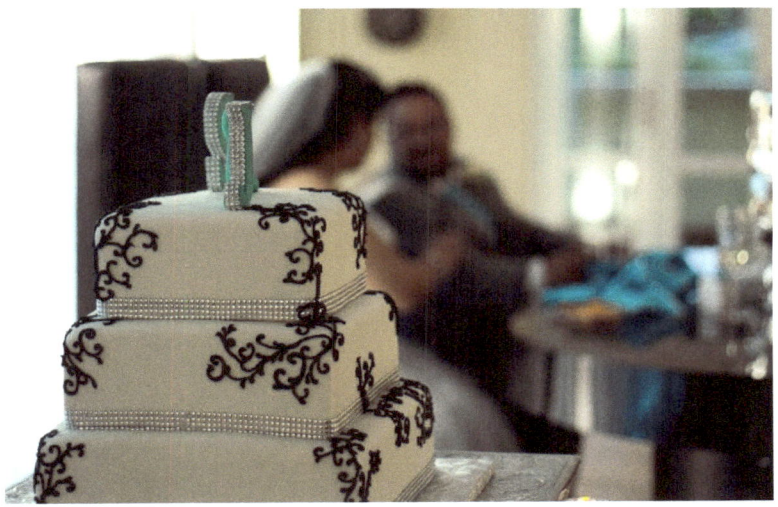

The wedding photojournalistic style is summed up in one word. "Moments". We do not focus to be attracting the attention of the couple. Otherwise, we want to be invisible to them. Eighty percent of our photos must be candid, while the other twenty will be posed photos. We have the duty to take photos throughout the day of the event to capture every one of the special moments. Yes, we should take posed photos, but this is not our focus. In the end, we are going to give the newlyweds a story of everything that happened on one of the most important days of their lives. They are going to thank us for forever.

PREPARATION

Once we are hired as photographers by the bride and groom, it means that they saw our portfolio and want to have spontaneous photos to remember the moments. They do 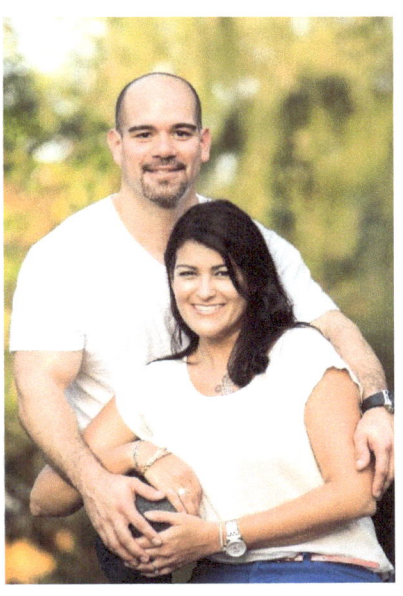 not want the photographer to be a nuisance on that day. Very few photos are going to be posed, but let's remember that we need to have a meeting with the bride and groom to tell us the photos that are essential for them, such as photos with specific family members and moments they want to have. This is important, because during the wedding day the bride and groom will be overwhelmed with many things in mind and will forget what was said in this meeting. So, it is our job to have the list on the wedding day and remember them everything. Being prepared as photographers for a wedding is of utmost importance so that we do not lack anything. Therefore, we must have everything ready the day before. I usually have a checklist for each of my weddings, in which I have everything necessary for my preparation in writing. Having a camera suitcase with wheels in which all our equipment fits would be ideal, to have everything in one place. In this way we sleep peacefully knowing that the next day everything will be ready.

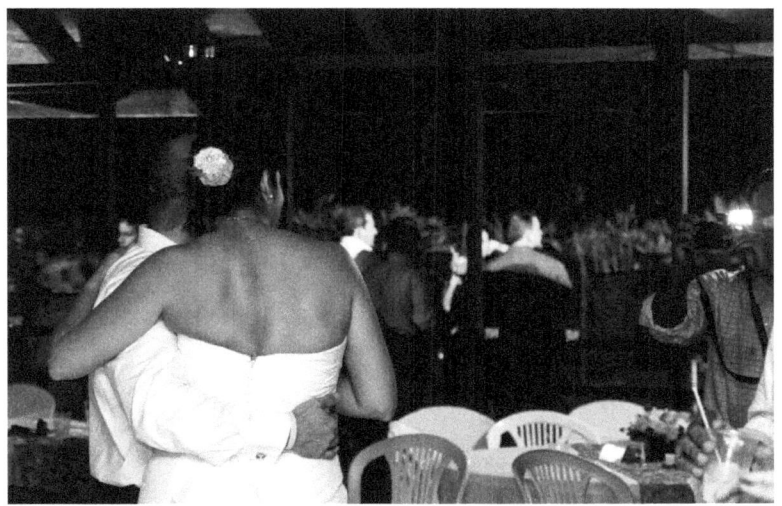

We must know the dressing code for the wedding, and we must dress as according to it. If the wedding is formal or casual, we will put on a nice suit and we will look elegant. If the wedding is on the beach, we will put on our flower shirt and shorts and let us look like fun.

AT THE BRIDE'S HOUSE

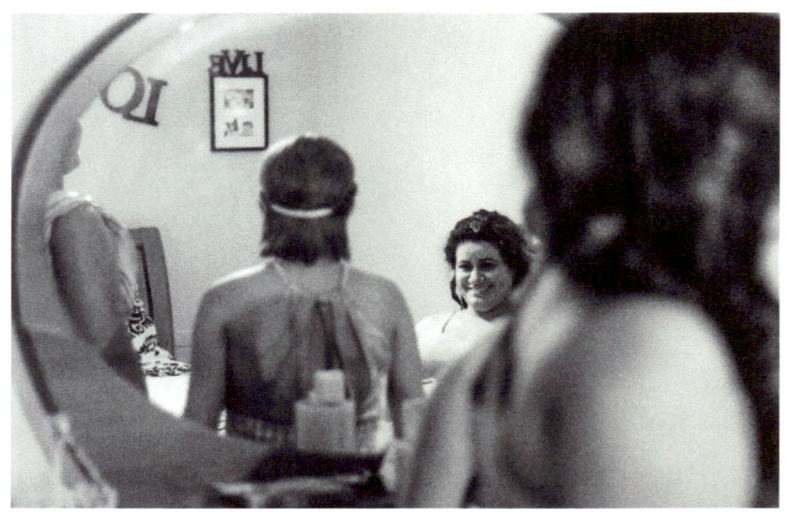

The first place that we will get first most of the time is to the bride's house. Here we must capture their preparation hours before the ceremony. We must arrive early. We are going to capture details of the moments of the preparation of the bride and her relatives, being us invisible.

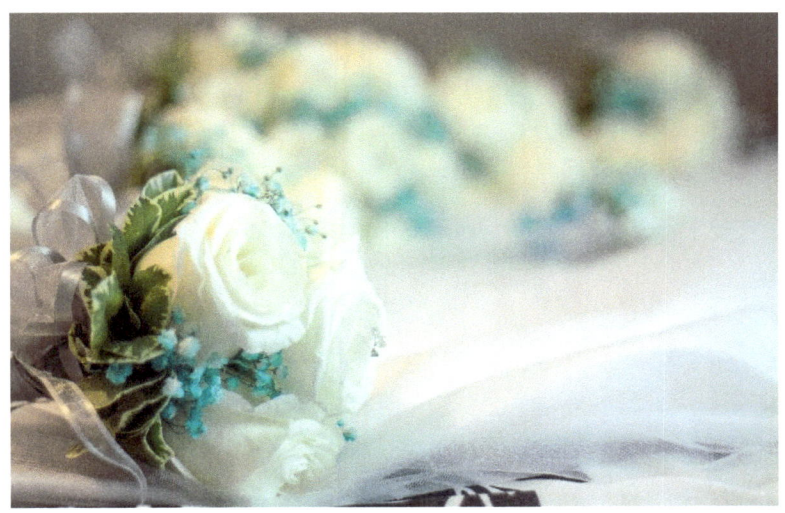

Let us take advantage of taking several photos of the flower bouquet.

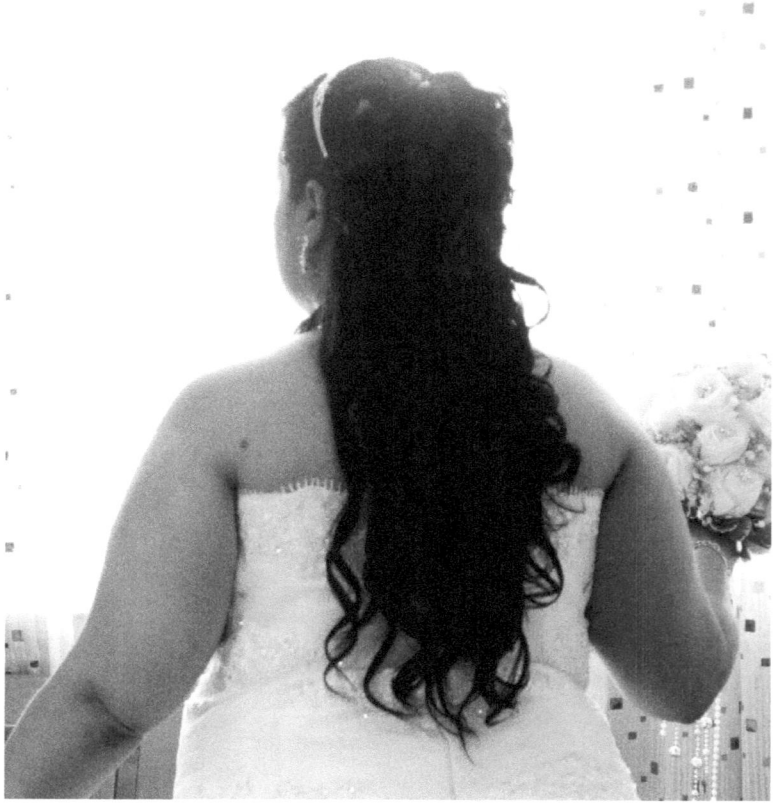

Finally, we can pose the bride alone and with her family.

GROOM

We are going to leave the bride's house directly to the place of the ceremony where we are going to meet with the groom. We are going to take some posed photos and then we are always aware of everything that happens around him.

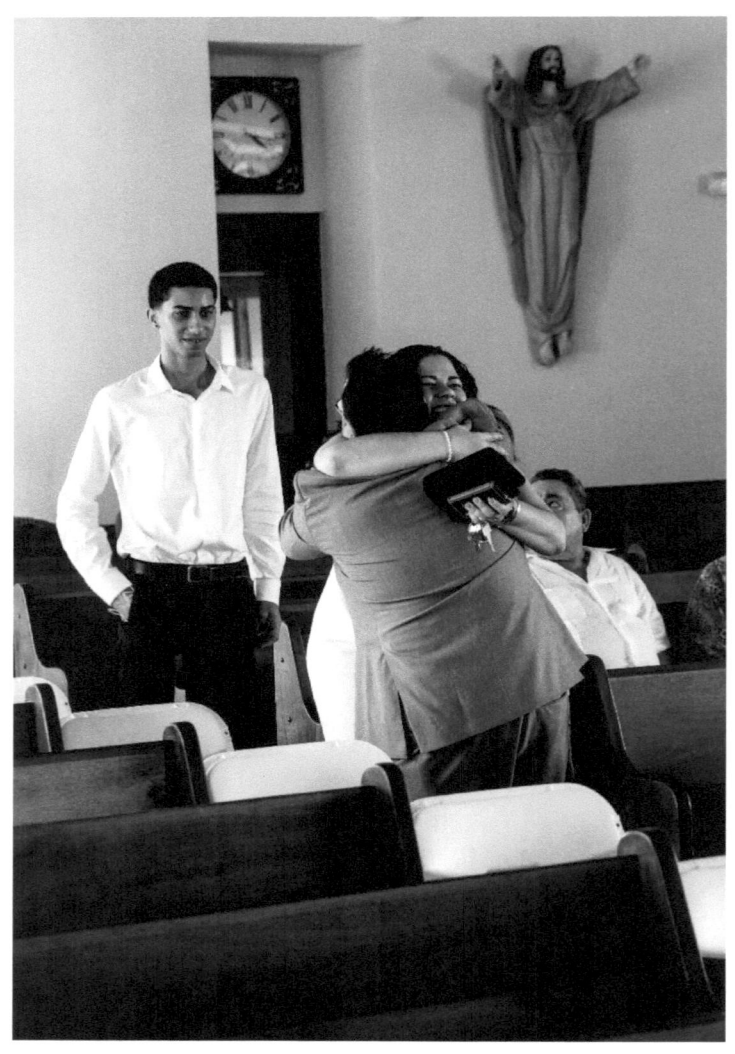

At this moment, a special relative arrived, and I managed to capture the moment.

CEREMONY

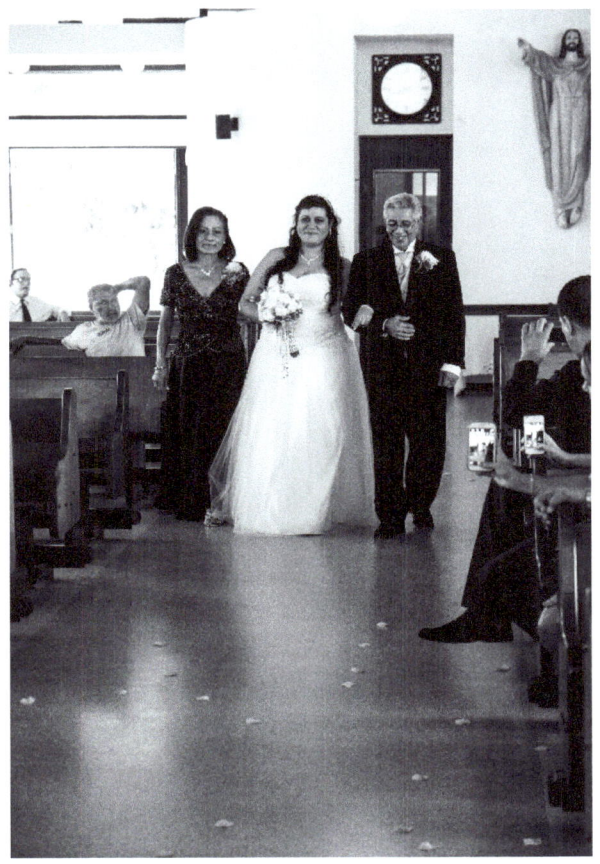

During the ceremony we will be awaiting the arrival of the bride at the church. Always attentive to funny moments, laughs and joys.

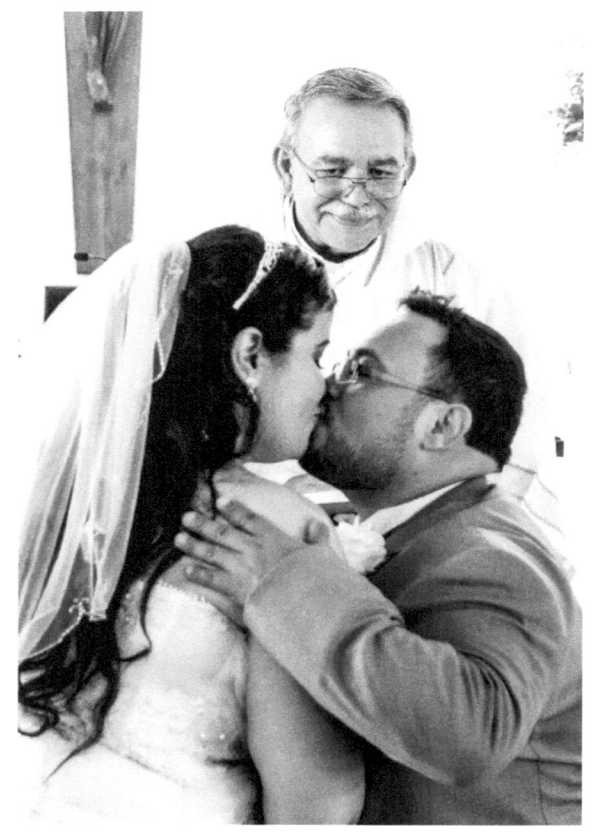

The moment of the kiss cannot be missed, so we must be at the correct angle and the exact moment. The camera should always be in Burst Mode so as not to miss the moment. At the end of the ceremony we are pending the list of requests of the bride and groom to remind them with whom they wanted to take posed photos.

RECEPTION

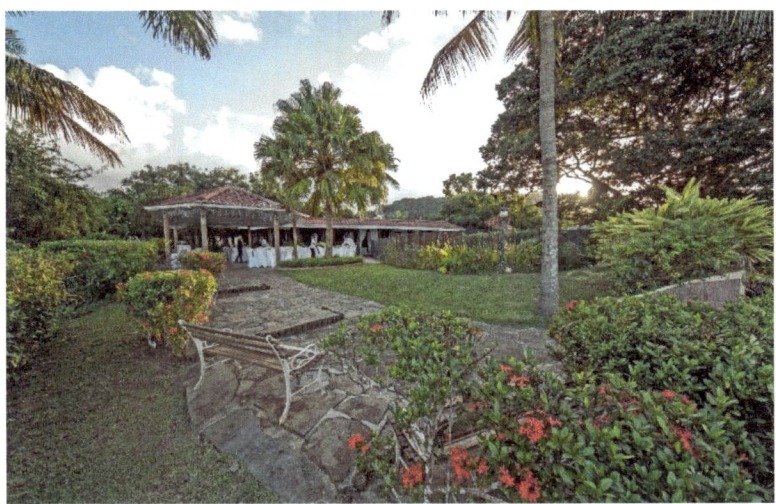

We will arrive early to the party place and we will wait for the newlyweds. We will take photos of the details like the reception place, tables, and some other interesting things.

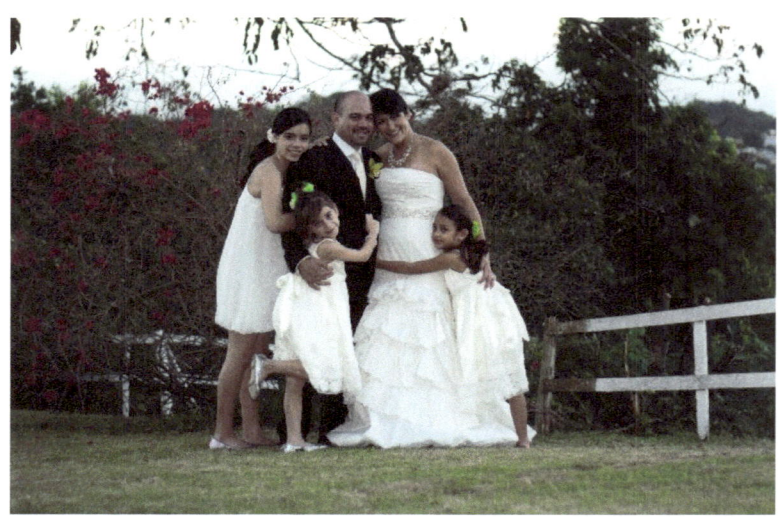

If we have the opportunity, we will take advantage of taking photos of the bride and groom outdoors, if the weather conditions allow it.

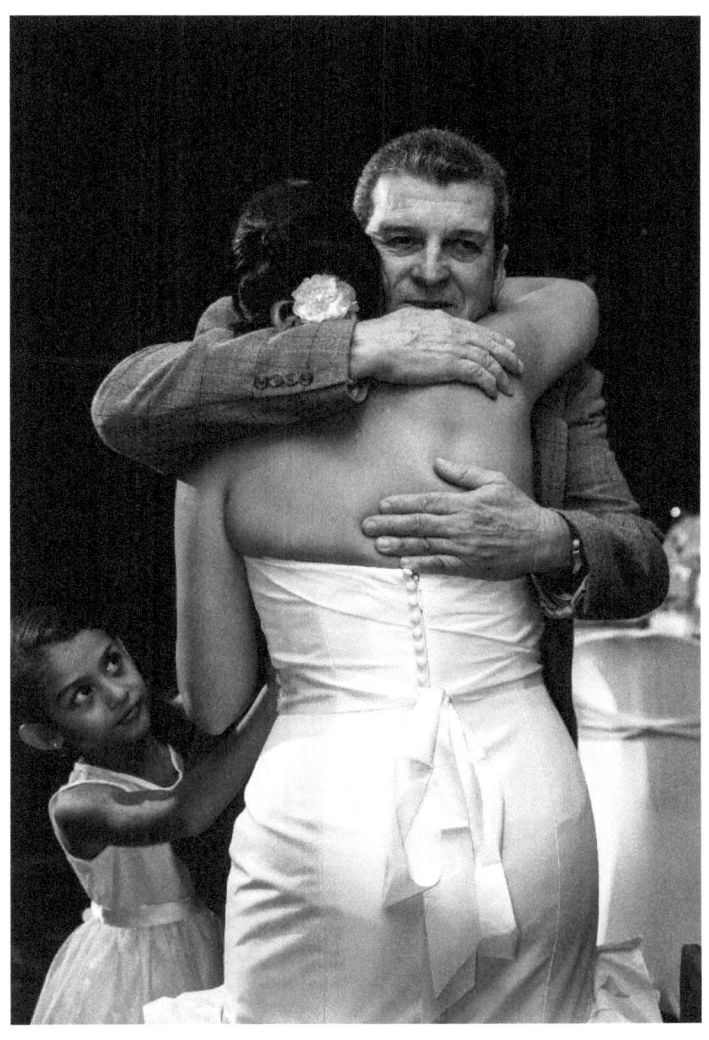

The arrival of some guests can be very emotional, so we must always be prepared.

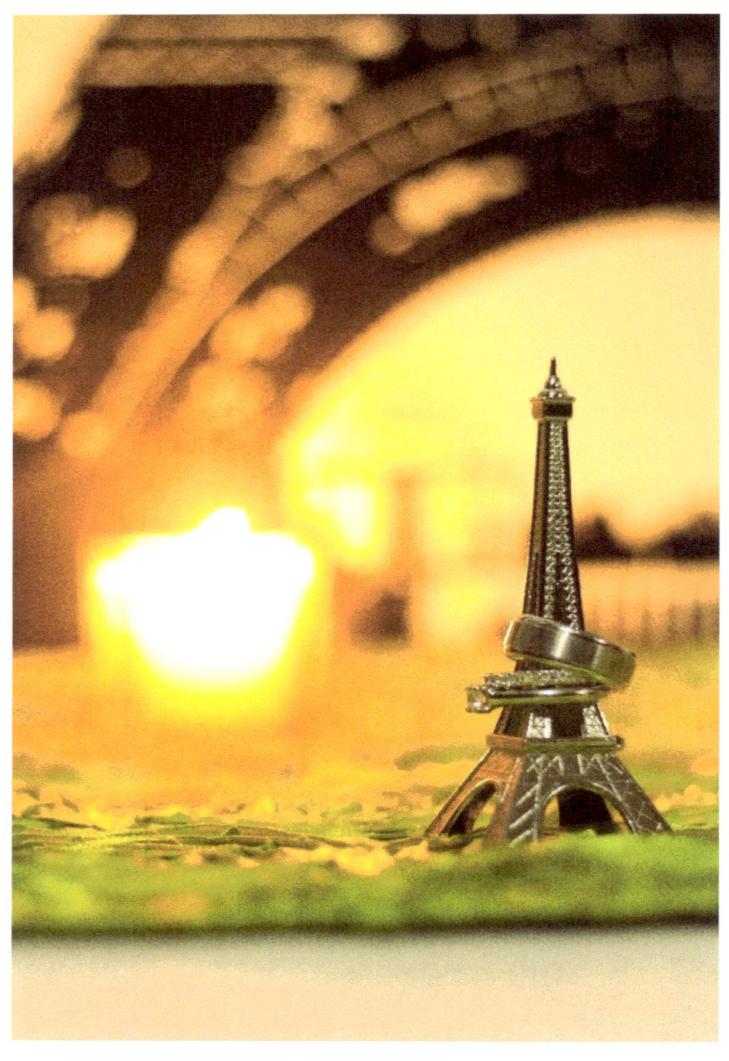

Taking a photo of the rings is very important.

CHILDREN

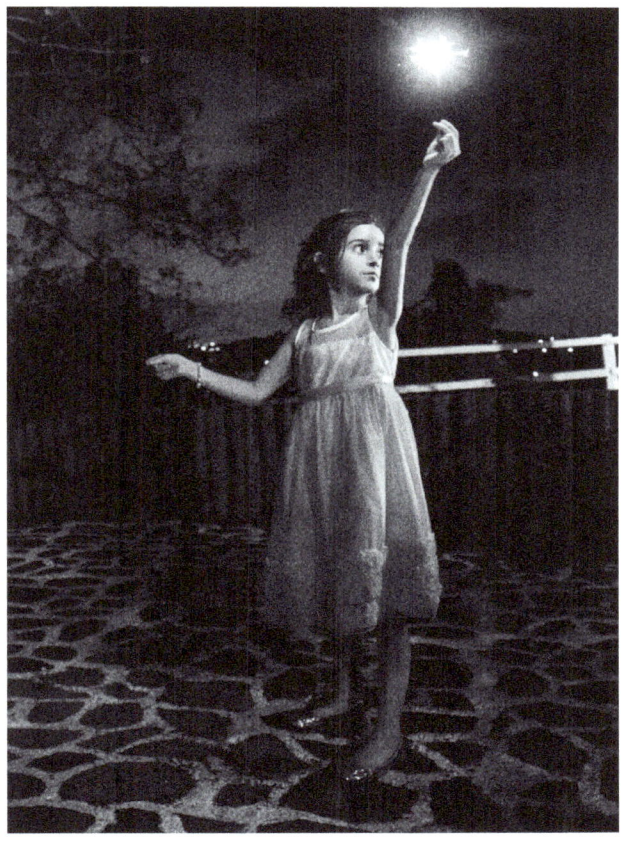

There are always children at weddings, and these are usually very naughty. Whenever we have the opportunity, we will take photos of them without them noticing. The bride and groom are going to thank us for these moments.

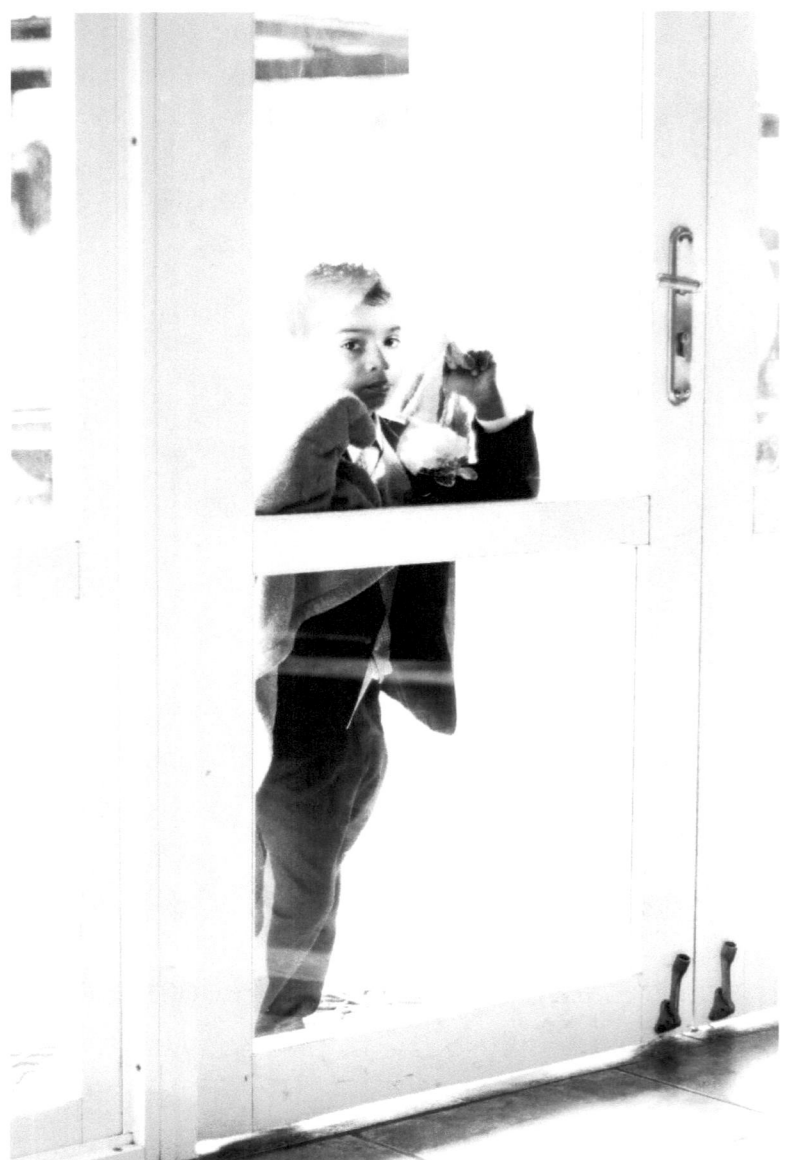

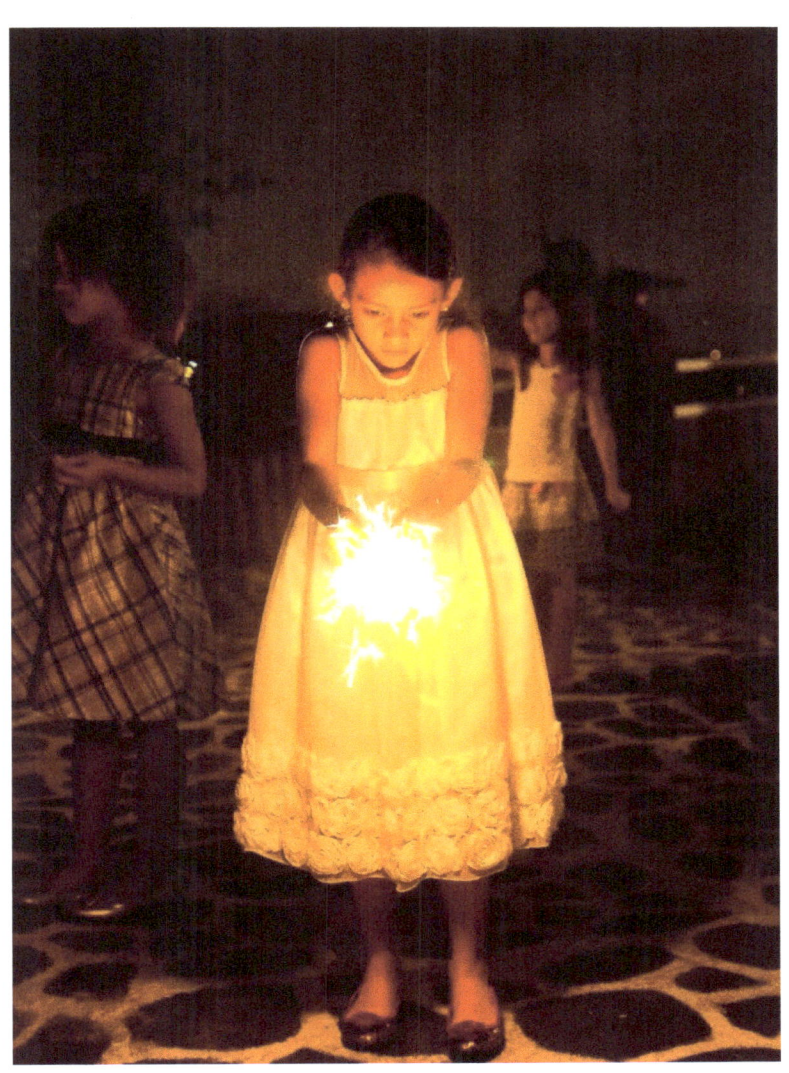

ACTION

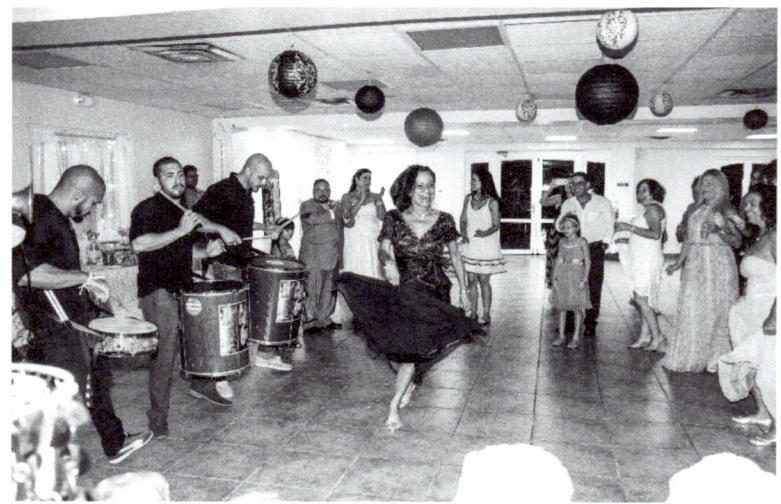

In most receptions there is music. And late at night guests tend to be more cheerful. At this time, we must have our camera in hand to capture the action. Our camera in burst mode will help us capture the perfect moment.

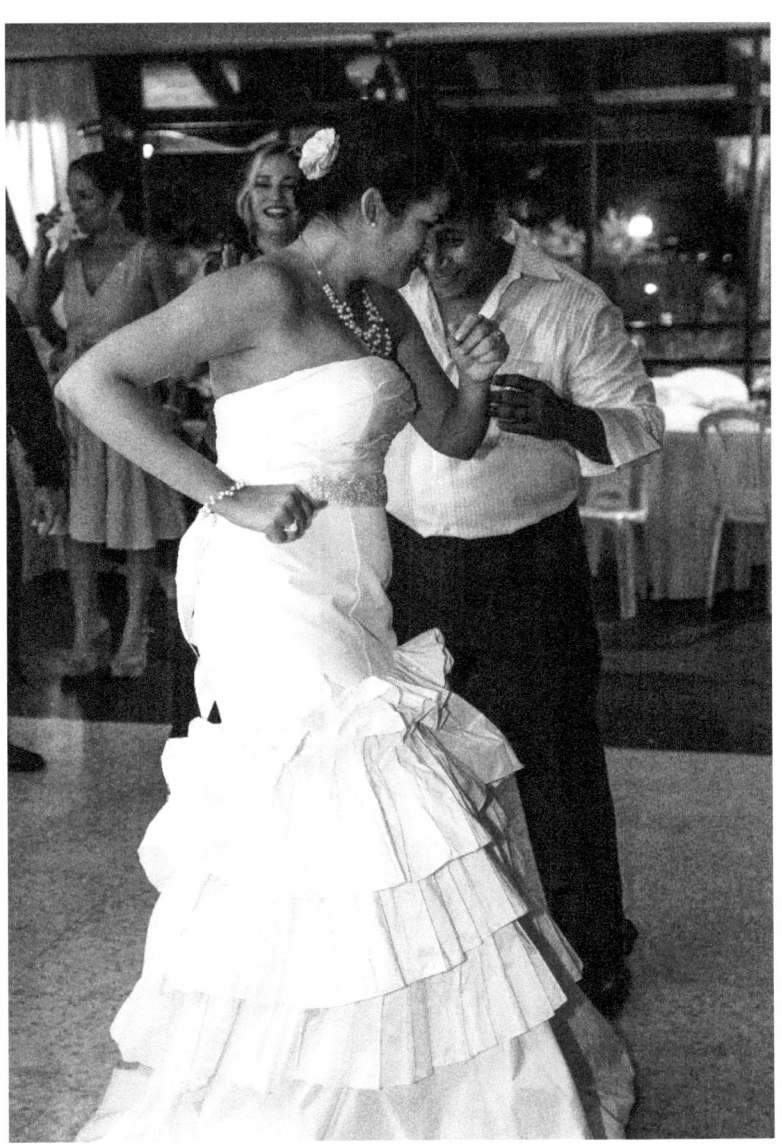

MOMENTS

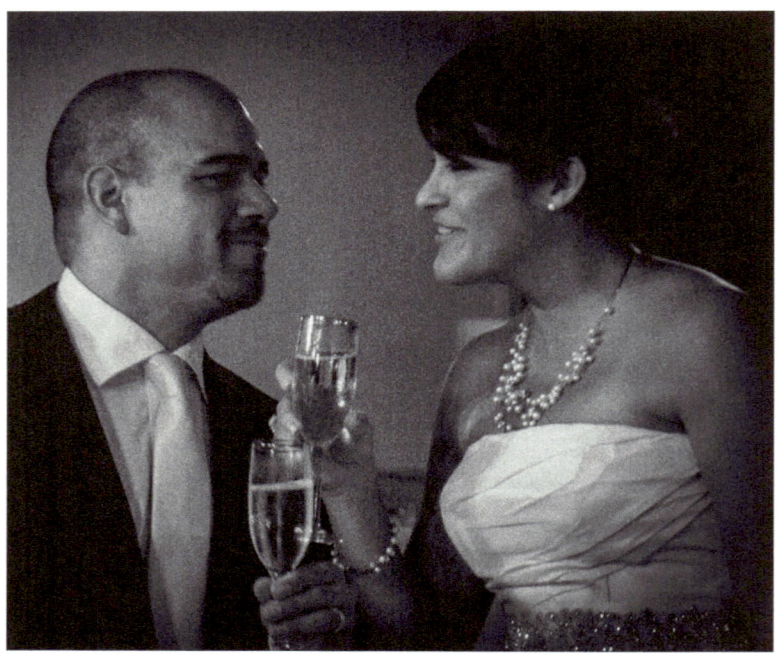

During the reception there are always special moments such as the waltz, toast, and the cut of the cake. We must be attentive to when they will occur so as not to miss the moment.

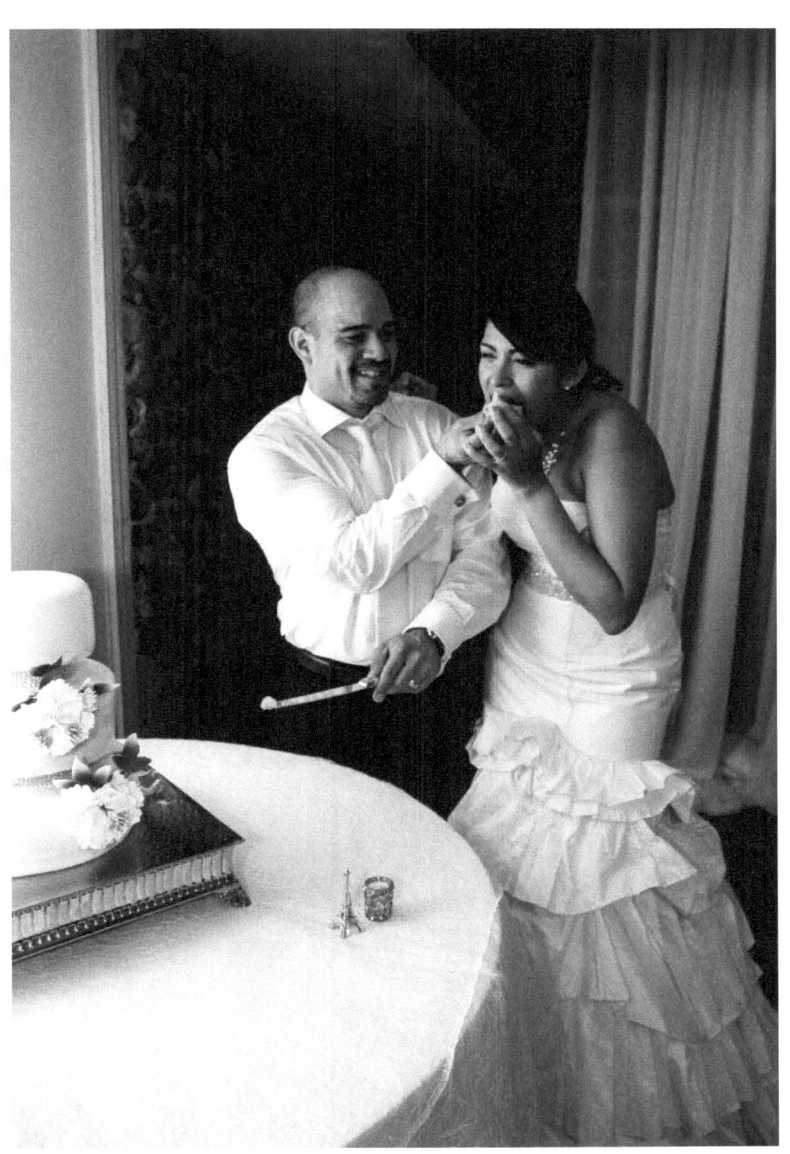

OTHER EVENTS

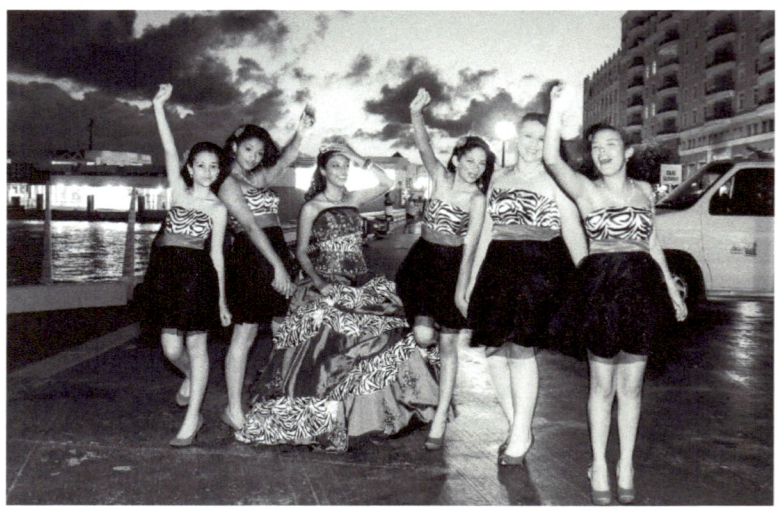

In addition to weddings, as photojournalistic photographers, we can also be hired for other types of events such as Sweet Sixteen.

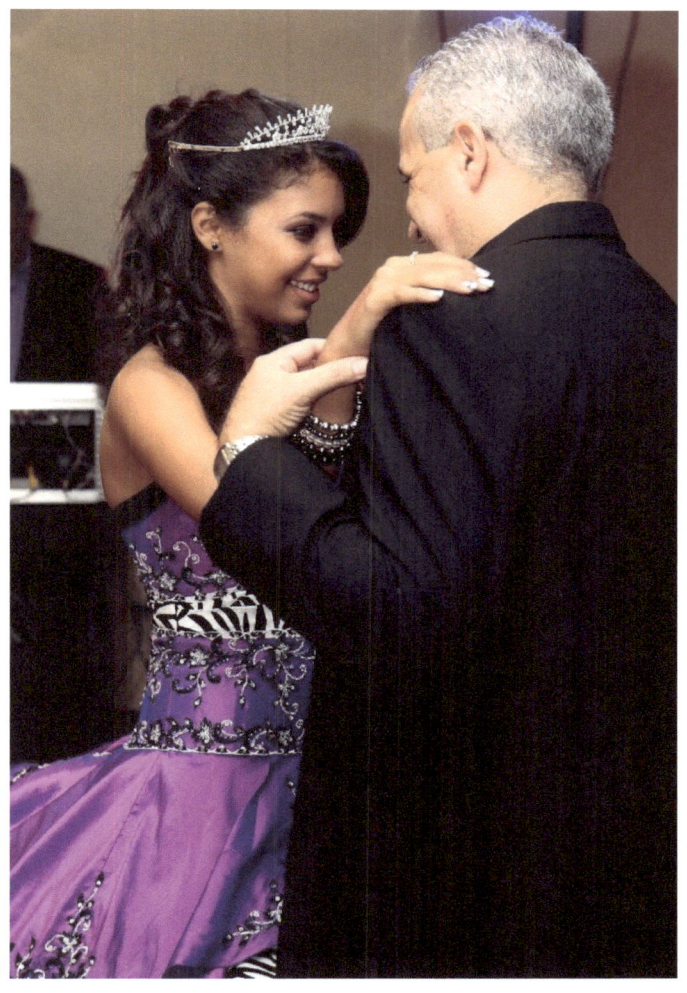

These events can be similar to weddings, so we can apply the same photo-journalistic style as we can see in this image.

LIGHT

At wedding events I work with natural light when we have good sunlight, and I work with an external flash when it is already night.

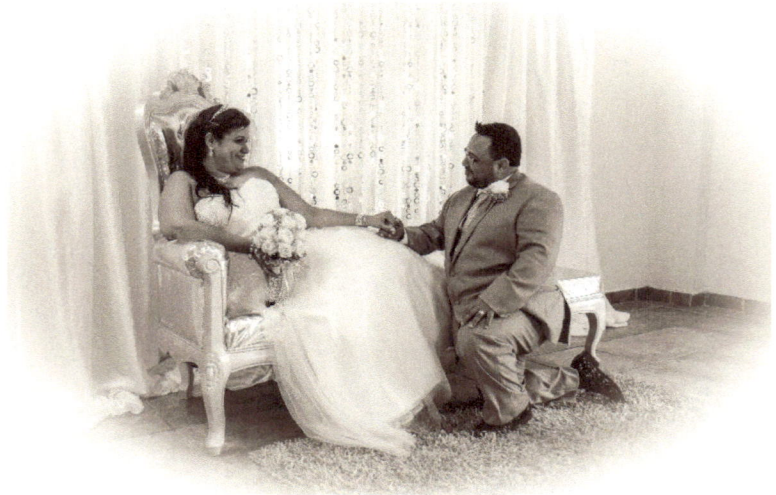

When we work with flash indoors, we must bounce the light off the ceiling or walls to avoid unwanted shadows.

TIPS FOR TAKING GREAT PHOTOS

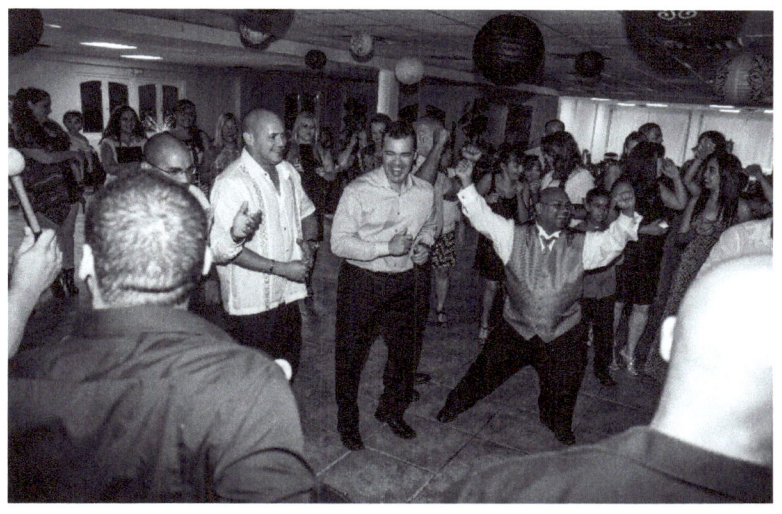

Let us always work with the camera in burst mode. In this way we try not to miss the perfect moment. Having two cameras on hand with two different lenses will help us with the varied artistic effect. We should never be concerned about running out of memory. These days memory cards are cheap. Let us buy memory cards with enough space and always have an extra card for security.

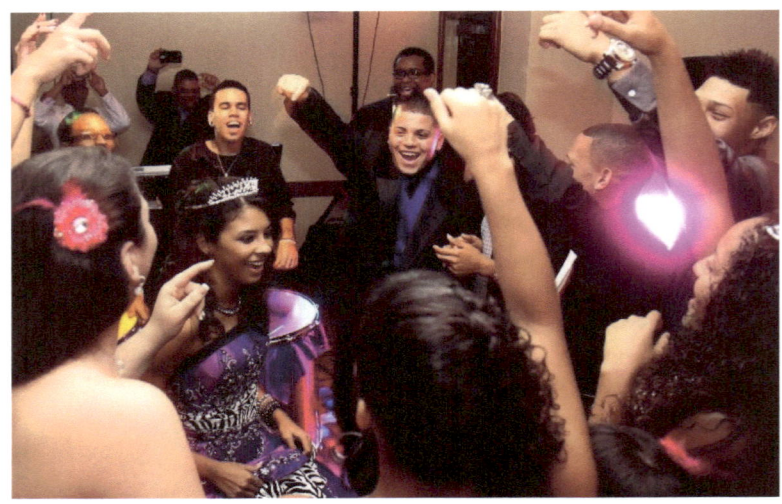

Always be ready for the moment, with both hands on the camera. Let us compose with our eye carefully and take the images. In this way we avoid spending more time editing. Remember that cropping too much reduces the resolution of the image.

EQUIPMENT

- Two DSLR cameras
- Telephoto Lens 28-70mm (for camera with full size sensor) or 17-50mm (for camera with APS-C sensor) with 2.8 fixed aperture at any distance and image stabilization
- Normal 50mm lens with maximum aperture of 1.8 or 1.4
- Battery grip for more power time and better camera handling
- Two memory cards with space for at least 2,000 images each
- 2 external "flash" with backup batteries
- Lens Cleaning Kit
- Lens Hood

CONTINGENCY PLANNING

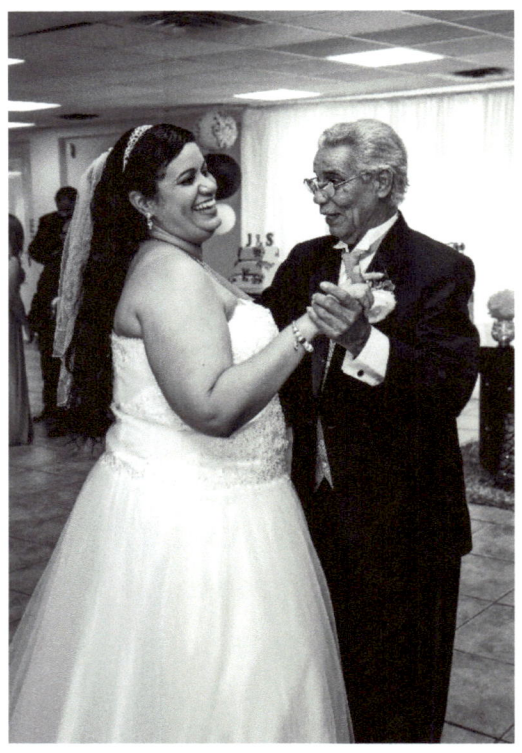

Backing up to a computer, external drive, and cloud service the next day of the event is a must. When editing, let us back up our work at the end every day. In this way we avoid losing our work in the event of any accident.

EDITING

My advice is to take all our photos in RAW format. This way we will have more control when editing. We can crop, adjust white balance, move up or down up to two full stops in case we lose the correct exposure due to light changes, and we can adjust shadows, highlights, and colors.

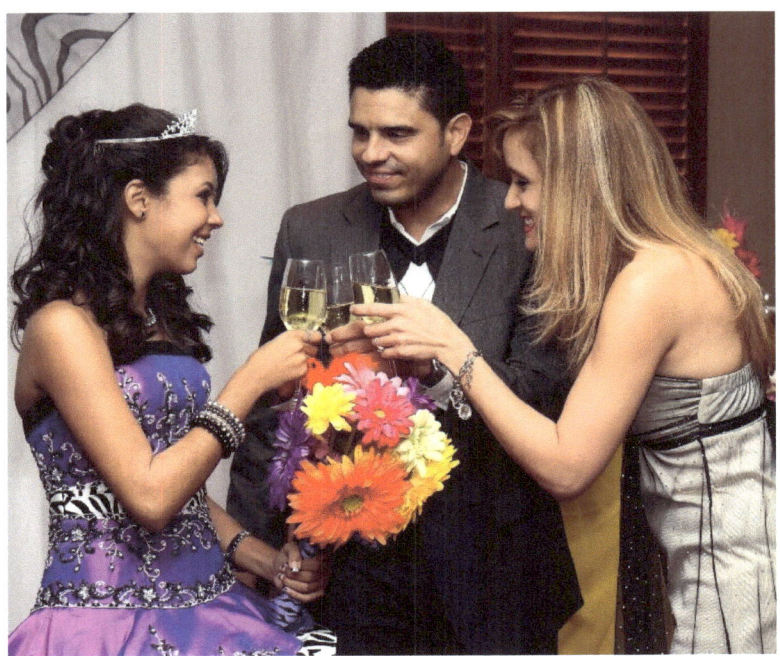

Photos in jpeg format are not very manageable. Use a good computer application to handle the RAW photo format. After we finish editing, we convert to the jpeg format for the final product.

FINAL PRODUCT

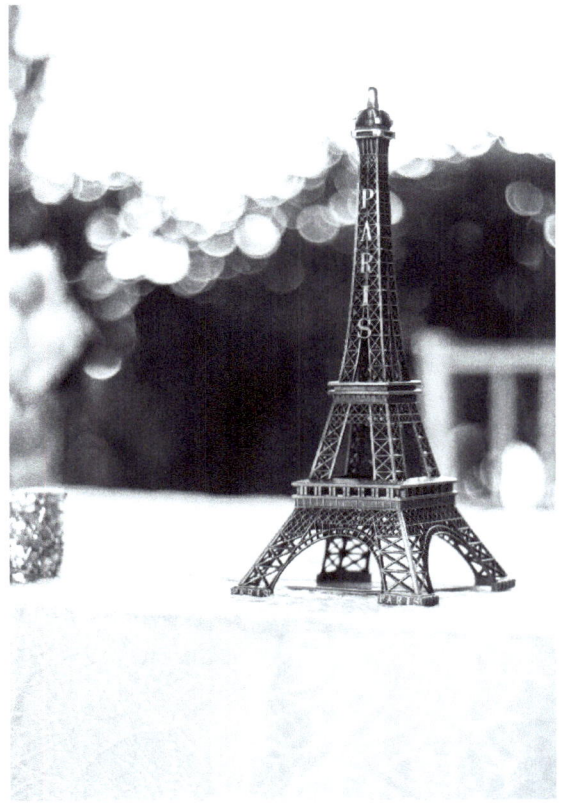

Because at weddings I always work with my camera in burst mode, I can end up with around 1500 photos per event. Already sitting in front of my computer, I begin to select the photos that artistically meet my requirements, and that will satisfy the needs of my clients. Then I start editing.

I deliver around 150 color images with black and white copies, on a well-presented device. On the Internet we can find several photography companies that help us with interesting articles and quality devices to store photos.

www.ingramcontent.com/pod-product-compliance
Lightning Source LLC
Chambersburg PA
CBHW040337220526
45473CB00009B/2711